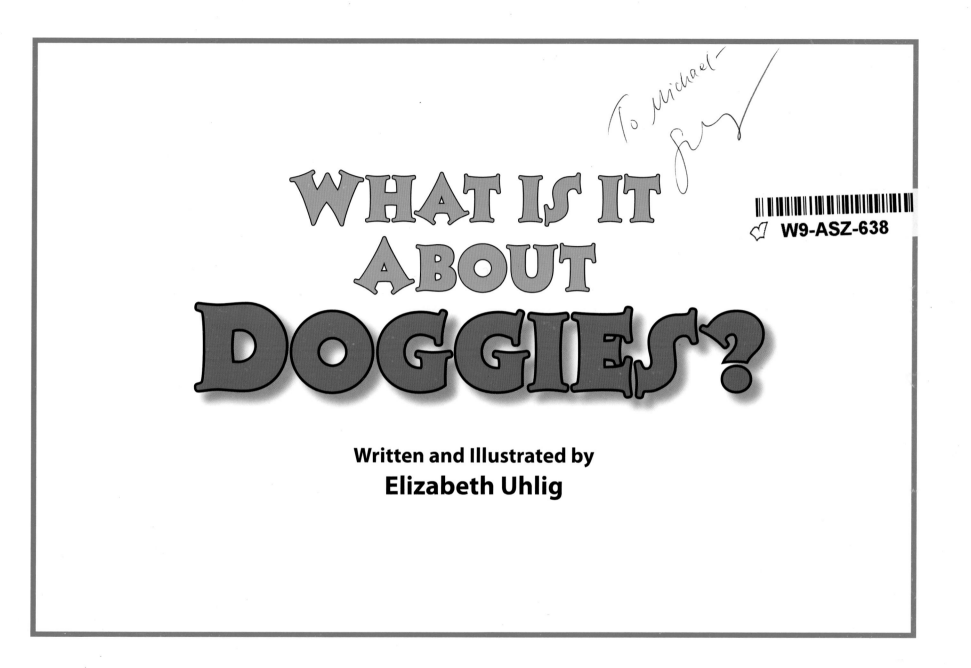

WHAT IS IT ABOUT DOGGIES?

Written and Illustrated by
Elizabeth Uhlig

Marble House Editions

Published by Marble House Editions
96-09 66th Avenue (Suite 1D)
Rego Park, NY 11374
elizabeth.uhlig@yahoo.com
www.marble-house-editions.com

Library of Congress Cataloguing-in-Publication Data
Uhlig, Elizabeth
What is it About Doggies?/ by Elizabeth Uhlig

<u>Summary</u>: A rhyming poem about dogs and why we love them.

ISBN 978-0-9834030-0-5
Library of Congress Catalog Card Number 20119059

Production Date   XXXX
Plant & Location   Printed by Everbest Printing Co. Ltd., Nansha, CHINA
Job & Batch # XXXX

This book is dedicated to my little friend Daniela,
and to animal lovers everywhere.

What is it about doggies?

Why do we love them so?

Why do we want to pet them?

Does anybody know?

Is it because they're friendly,

and want to say hello?

Or perhaps because they're funny and get cuter as they grow.

3

Doggies are so curious! They want to know what's what.

They always like to have a treat — anything you've got!

They really like to cuddle,

6

...and of course they want to play!

And even when they're naughty,
we love them anyway.

8

Some dogs are just plain beautiful. Some are fancy, too.

And some are very tiny and can fit right in a shoe!

We must never, ever harm them,  but treat them carefully,

...make sure they get just what they need,

12

...and keep them company!

My neighborhood is full of dogs, and none belong to me,

but still, each one is special, as you shall quickly see.

There's Dumpling and there's Pumpkin,

There's Bauer and there's Box.

There's Tootsie and there's Pickle,

18

There's Maizie and there's Socks.

There's Louie and there's Lola,

There's Lucky, Max and Blue.

There's Bixie and her sister, Scout,

22

…and little Otto, too!

Stitch and Sam are brothers,

24

...and Cody is a mutt.

Disco is quite fussy,
and so is Suzy, but....

It really doesn't matter,
I want them ALL, you see,

…and if I could, I'd take them home,
and keep them just for me.

What ***is*** it about doggies?

It's their very special knack —

We always want to
love them . . .

'cause they *always* love us back.